Does your life on fast forward?

Do you notice that as you've got older, that time seems to speed up?

Perhaps years don't seem quite as long as before? Do you go from birthday to birthday and wonder where all the time has gone? Or travel somewhere and hardly remember anything of the journey? Or have a meal while watching television and hardly notice the taste and smells of the food?

Is life passing you by - and you're not fully taking part? Does it ever feel like you're on automatic - going through the motions each day, surviving but not really living?

Are you so focused on doing and getting through that there's no time for you to really live - to slow down, and notice the details of each moment?

Q. What big and small things in your life might you be overlooking?
a). Experiences

b). People

LIVING LIFE TO THE FULL OR LIVING LIFE TOO FAST?

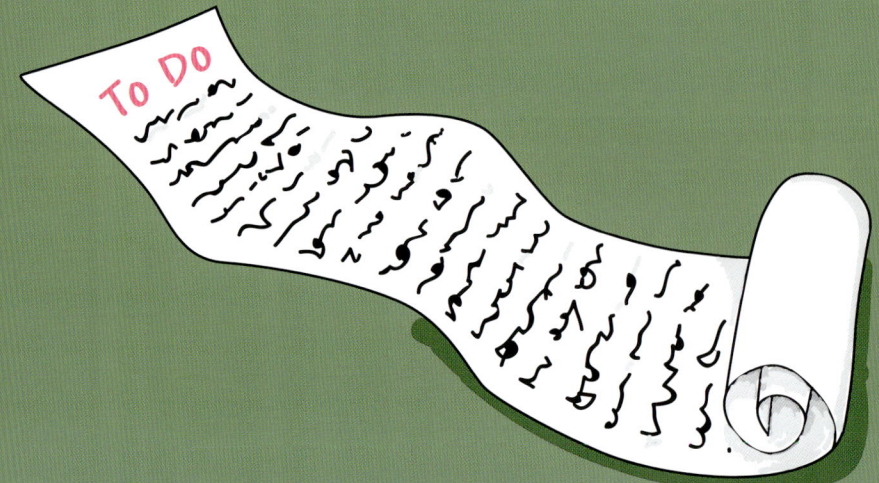

Are you rushing through every day?

Whether it's the pressure of helping children get ready for school, or the demands to do, do, do - does each day seem relentless with a To-Do list that never runs out?

Chasing the clock and feeling under pressure all the time stimulates the same fight or flight survival responses in our body that being threatened by a wild animal or an oncoming car creates.

Whatever is going on, are you so busy you don't have time for You? Are you doing things all the time with no time for rest, perhaps working through lunch, giving time to help others but not yourself?

Q. Is your life all about do, do, do? What fills it?

Q. What stops you from taking time to stop, think and reflect?

Q. Are there any down sides of being so busy
- for you?

- for others?

LIFE EVENTS AND HASSLES

Perhaps we are struggling with a small number of very large life pressures and demands such as debt? Or a problem relationship? Or maybe life seems to be a series of smaller hassles all the time?

We can often cope when we face just one or two small hassles. Things like having the shopping to do and there's no time. Putting the sheets out to dry, then it rains and we're out of the house? It's not a crisis, but just an added hassle. One hassle at a time may seem fine, but too many one after another can grind anyone down.

Q. What (if any) large life events are you currently facing?
_____
_____

Q. Does it seem life is full of smaller hassles? Like what?
_____
_____

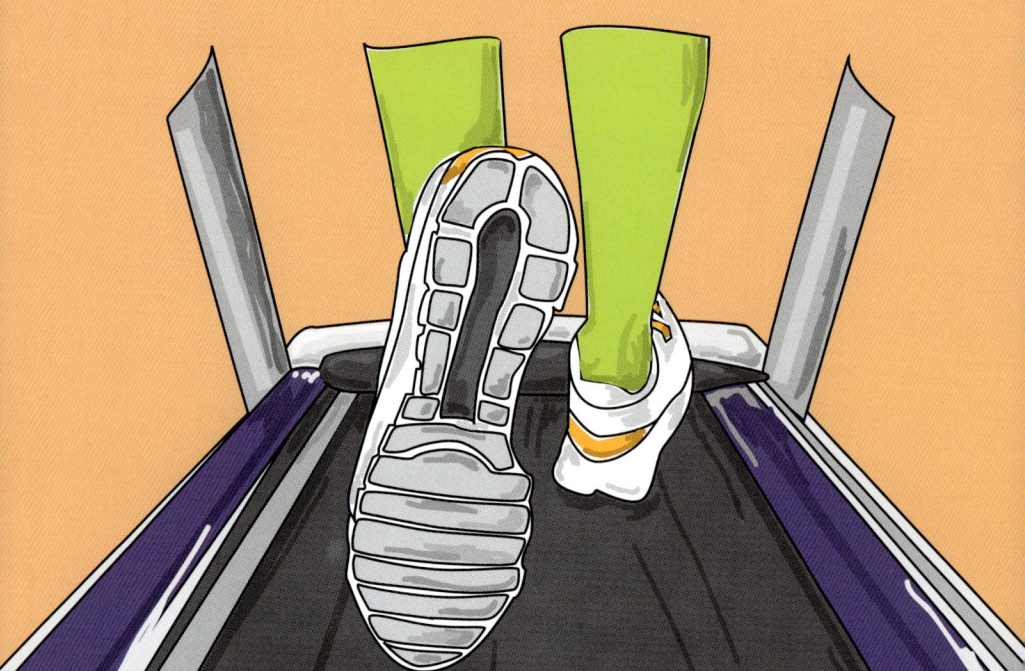

Get beyond the fantasy

Maybe sometimes you need to make a change. Get a new job? Walk away from a difficult situation?

It's tempting to look for easy solutions. An escape route like a lottery ticket that will change everything fast.

But it's a fantasy.

Mindfulness aims to help you see things as they really are and start from there.

It's not about avoiding things or emptying your mind. It's about moving your attention so that you can start to see your problems with a bit more perspective. Seeing things with clarity, not distorted or exaggerated or coloured by emotion. It will allow you to respond to things wisely, with more skillfulness and strategy giving yourself time to trust your judgment

If you slow down, step back and observe, you're far more likely to come up with a helpful solution. Something that is realistic not a fantasy.

HERE'S A BETTER SOLUTION*

* and anyone can do it.

You can create more space in life using an approach called mindfulness

You're going to learn how to:
1. Pay attention to the right stuff, not just the hassles and pressures that shout out and demand attention.
2. Slow down so that you can calmly see what's happening more clearly.
3. Practice kindness to yourself and others.

When we feel under pressure we often start to say things to ourselves that aren't very nice. We become self-critical or even hate ourselves as well as the situation. So if that's you, now's the time to do something different and choose to practice being kinder to yourself.

You also need to look inside and discover more about what's really going on. What's your inner voice saying? Is it a critic, or a supporter?

This book offers a gift - it will help you really get to know yourself in a kinder way. You'll also learn to live life in a fuller way.

THE ORIGINS OF MINDFULNESS

An approach to life

Many people may associate mindfulness with practices from a Buddhist tradition. Mindfulness certainly is an important aspect of Buddhist practice, however all of the world's great religions have used reflection and meditation as key parts of their faith over the millennia.

Mindfulness techniques are also used for their own benefits, separate from any spiritual practices. Slowing down and peaceful reflection is something that can benefit everyone whether they have a faith or none.

DON'T TALK YOURSELF OUT OF CHANGE

What are you thinking?

One of the big reasons people don't choose to make changes in life is they don't believe it's possible. What about you? Have you noticed any of the following doubts or fears?

1. *I won't be able to do it.*
   Did you ever learn to ride a bike, swim or drive a car? Maybe that seemed difficult too at the time?

2. *I don't have the time.*
   Mindfulness is an attitude that can be part of your everyday life.

3. *It won't work for me.*
   You can travel a long way on any journey - but you need to take it one step at a time. Like most skills, you need to practice what you will learn again and again so it becomes second nature.

4. *It sounds like some sort of dodgy "alternative therapy" thing.*
   National treatment guidelines take a hard look at the evidence and recommend mindfulness to help prevent recurrent depression.*

5. *I've been told mindfulness is against my religious beliefs.*
   Most major religions have important meditation, reflection and contemplative elements. The approaches we teach you here are compatible for use whatever your own faith practice or none.

* Visit nice.org.uk to review current guidelines, or visit Mindfulness Scotland www.mindfulnessscotland.org.uk

WHAT YOU ARE GOING TO LEARN?

About our approach

The mindfulness approach we will teach has three aspects. It invites you to choose to make an active choice to:

1. Pay attention
2. Slow down your life
3. Practice being kind

BUT FIRST LET'S LOOK AT HOW OUR MIND WORKS

Terrified of Heights! Heart racing! Going to collapse! Too much to do. If I can't sleep I'll feel awful. Going to be sick! Can't breathe! Can't cope. Going to make a fool out of myself! Going to be sick! Can't breathe!

Change your thinking, change your brain

When we worry about things it changes our bodies too. Mental tension leads to physical tension in our bodies, so that it feels like we are running a marathon all day long.

What you might not know is you can often detect the physical impact of stress and low mood in blood tests and brain scans. Our brains literally change when we face long-term stress. Mindfulness helps you to re-wire your brain, weaken unhelpful worry habits and improve your body stress chemicals and hormones too.

But you can't change what you don't know - so the first step is to start to become more aware of your thoughts, body and reactions.

BEING AWARE OF YOUR THOUGHTS: LET'S PLAY DETECTIVE

Think about a situation:

Imagine someone is stuck in traffic. They need to get somewhere important, but are going to be late.

How might they react? Thinking, feelings, in their bodies or in their actions?

Perhaps someone in that situation might think "It's terrible I'll be late", "What will people think?" "It will be so embarrassing going into the meeting after it's started", "I'm so annoyed at these workmen mending the road!" or "Why is the driver in front going so slowly!" ... if they thought like this, then they might feel low, anxious, angry or ashamed. Or maybe even guilty - "I've let them down because I set off late".

The strong emotions might affect how they feel physically - feeling hot, tension in the head, tight stomach, achy, or perhaps feeling sick when they think about the consequences. And all this might add up to affect their behaviour. So maybe they sound their horn loudly, or try to phone ahead while they drive, shouting and swearing under their breath. These thoughts and reactions can quickly affect how the person feels.

Key Point: What they think affects how they feel and what they do.

In fact, our emotions and reactions can spin like a cycle.

HERE'S A DIAGRAM THAT HELPS US UNDERSTAND WHAT'S HAPPENING

Example: The vicious cycle quickly spins...

* Download from www.llttf.com/resources

1. What's going on? Describe the situation:
Stuck in traffic and going to be late for a very important meeting.

Altered Thinking
2. My thoughts:
I'll be late. This is terrible. What will people think. The road works are messing things up!

Altered Feelings
3. My feelings:
Angry, stressed, guilty.

Altered Behaviour
5. My behaviour:
Rev the engine. Hoot the horn. Hit the steering wheel. Swear at the driver ahead.

Altered Physical Feelings
4. My body:
Physical tension. Rapid, shallow breathing. Heart rate increases.

As the cycle spins we feel worse and worse. So, how do you stop things spinning out of control?

* Linked resources are available for free online.

23

NOW BRING TO MIND A TIME WHEN YOU FELT UPSET OR STRESSED

Think back over the last day or two to a time that's felt difficult. Something mildly difficult, not catastrophic or overwhelming.

Use the diagram on the right to begin to tease out and untangle what was happening.

The vicious cycle

1. What's going on? Describe the situation:

Altered Thinking
2. My thoughts:

Altered Feelings
3. My feelings:

Altered Behaviour
5. My behaviour:

Altered Physical Feelings
4. My body:

This happens so quickly - the cycle spins. So, how do you stop things spinning out of control?

WHAT YOU ARE GOING TO LEARN

.... AND HOW YOU WILL KNOW IT HELPS

What we think powerfully affects how we feel and what we do. Notice your own reactions when you feel stressed or tense. You may become aware of patterns that repeat. For example, noticing a tension headache, breathing faster, feeling fidgety, snapping at other people, noticing an upset stomach or tightness or tension in the chest, or becoming avoidant or pushing people away.

In the same way that we often experience repeating physical patterns at times when we feel stressed, we can also notice repeating patterns of stressful thinking that occur again and again whenever we feel a strongly negative emotion.

These types of unhelpful thinking patterns have a negative impact on how we feel and on what we do.

If you are interested in finding out more about unhelpful thinking and the impact of how this affects us, visit www.llttf.com.

YOU ARE NOT YOUR THOUGHTS

Pay attention
(skills 1,2,3)

Slow down your life
(skills 4,5,6)

Practice being kind
(skills 7,8,9)

How this course will work:

The next few pages will teach a range of new skills:

Pay attention:
How to respond differently when you start to notice your thoughts spinning out of control.

Slow down your life:
So you can really see what's happening.

Practice being kind:
To yourself. To others. By expressing thanks for the positives in our lives.

The next pages teach new skills in all three of these areas.

HERE'S HOW TO BREAK THE CYCLE

BEFORE

WHAT ARE YOU AWARE OF JUST NOW?
- ☐ My breathing
- ☐ My body
- ☐ My feelings
- ☐ My thoughts
- ☐ My actions

SELF-REFLECTION:

Example:
Don't complete this just now.

Pay attention (skills 1,2,3)

This next section teaches you three skills to help you move your mind away from the cycle of worry that makes you feel worse and worse.

You will learn:
1. To ground yourself.
2. To be aware of your breathing.
3. To pay attention to your body.

Choosing to shift your attention in this way gives your mind a chance to settle and rest.

But first, before you start to practice how to make changes, let us introduce you to a way of reflecting on the impact of the new mindfulness skills you will learn. Before and after you try a new skill, we suggest you record what you notice is going on in your body and mind. Use the Before box to help you reflect, and then re-visit this After each new mindfulness practice. Mindfulness can help you become more aware of your inner experiences as a starting point for change.

AFTER

WHAT ARE YOU AWARE OF JUST NOW?	SELF-REFLECTION:
☐ My breathing ☐ My body ☐ My feelings ☐ My thoughts ☐ My actions	*Example: Don't complete this just now.* If things have altered, is this something you would like to plan to practice? Y ☐ N ☐

Skill 1
Pay attention

GROUND YOURSELF*

skills 1,2,3

BEFORE	WHAT ARE YOU AWARE OF JUST NOW? ☐ My breathing ☐ My body ☐ My feelings ☐ My thoughts ☐ My actions	SELF-REFLECTION:

* Hint - try walking with bare feet and experience the sensations of carpet, grass etc.

When your mind is full of thoughts spinning round and round, and making you feel worse, the first key thing to do is to stop and move your attention away from the racing thoughts. See this as actively choosing what to focus on. It's not about avoidance or running away. Instead, focus on the part of your body furthest away from your head - the soles of your feet.

Skill 1. Gather, Ground and Go forward:
Pay attention to your feet. Place both feet flat on the floor. Feel the soles of your feet inside your shoes. Notice any pressure, or warmth or coolness in your feet. Be curious about the sensations. What is noticed? Feel the contact of your socks and shoes. Any tingling or tightness? Any comfortable or uncomfortable sensations? What about the ground you stand on? Is it flat or on an incline, smooth or bumpy? What sensations do you notice in your ankles and muscles of your feet? A download is available for you to use.

Key Point: Every time your mind tugs you away from your feet and back to the spinning cycle, gently redirect your focus back to your feet. This gives your mind a rest.

AFTER

WHAT ARE YOU AWARE OF JUST NOW? ☐ My breathing ☐ My body ☐ My feelings ☐ My thoughts ☐ My actions	SELF-REFLECTION: If things have altered, is this something you would like to plan to practice? Y ☐ N ☐

Skill 2
Pay attention

FOCUS ON YOUR BREATHING

skills 1,2,3

BEFORE

WHAT ARE YOU AWARE OF JUST NOW?
- ☐ My breathing
- ☐ My body
- ☐ My feelings
- ☐ My thoughts
- ☐ My actions

SELF-REFLECTION:

Here's how to focus on your breathing*

- Find a quiet place, and a comfortable and supportive way to sit.
- Drop your shoulders and feel your feet or legs on the ground.
- Begin to bring your attention to your breathing.
- You might like to follow the cycle of breathing starting at your nose and mouth. Observe the air entering and leaving. Really be aware of the cool dry air entering, and the warm air leaving.
- Bring attention to your upper chest, to your side ribs and to the area above and behind your belly button.

To follow the whole journey of the breath, we have prepared different downloads (male and female voices with shorter and longer versions) you can use to help you practice this process.

Remember your mind will wander as you do this. This isn't a mistake, it's normal and not wrong.

AFTER

WHAT ARE YOU AWARE OF JUST NOW?	SELF-REFLECTION:
☐ My breathing ☐ My body ☐ My feelings ☐ My thoughts ☐ My actions	
	If things have altered, is this something you would like to plan to practice? Y ☐ N ☐

*It's all about noticing, rather than thinking changing or fixing.

Skill 3

Pay attention

FOCUS ON YOUR BODY

skills 1,2,3

BEFORE

WHAT ARE YOU AWARE OF JUST NOW?
- ☐ My breathing
- ☐ My body
- ☐ My feelings
- ☐ My thoughts
- ☐ My actions

SELF-REFLECTION:

We invite you now to experience a body scan. The audio download will guide you through your body bringing attention to each area in turn.

The intention of this practice is to help you to begin to develop a friendly way of connecting with your body.

- Your body scan is not primarily about relaxation, although that may occur as an off-shoot.
- It aims to help wake up to the sensations and experiences in your body right now.

You may not be aware of many of the messages your body is trying to pass on to you.

Use the downloads (again with shorter and longer versions) to help you develop your ability to really experience your body scan.

AFTER

WHAT ARE YOU AWARE OF JUST NOW?	SELF-REFLECTION:
☐ My breathing ☐ My body ☐ My feelings	
☐ My thoughts ☐ My actions	If things have altered, is this something you would like to plan to practice? Y ☐ N ☐

37

Skill 4
Slow down your life

MINDFUL EATING

skills 4, 5, 6

BEFORE

WHAT ARE YOU AWARE OF JUST NOW?
- ☐ My breathing
- ☐ My body
- ☐ My feelings
- ☐ My thoughts
- ☐ My actions

SELF-REFLECTION:

Join the campaign for slow eating

Mindful eating: Food is amazing, full of colours, textures and flavours. However, how often do you eat without attention without really noticing the meal?

Pay attention to where and how you eat. Set a place at the table. Make it a special time. Look and smell before you eat, then be aware of what you eat. Slow it down and savour the process. Bring your senses to your meal times. What are you feeding yourself? Chew slowly - really taste. Sense the textures. Put your knife and fork down between bites. No phones, technology or TV.

Mindful cooking: Is preparing a meal all about ready meals/fast food, or do you ever cook from scratch? Can you prioritise cooking at least once more a week so cooking becomes a time of enjoyment and nourishment?

Mindful shopping: Once you pay more attention to what you eat, you might notice it changes what you buy also.

AFTER

WHAT ARE YOU AWARE OF JUST NOW?
- ☐ My breathing
- ☐ My body
- ☐ My feelings
- ☐ My thoughts
- ☐ My actions

SELF-REFLECTION:

If things have altered, is this something you would like to plan to practice?   Y ☐ N ☐

Download from www.llttf.com/resources

Skill 5
Slow down your life

MINDFUL LISTENING

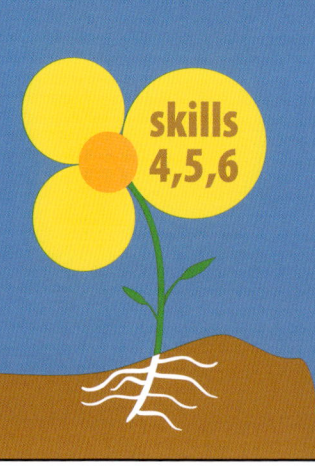

skills 4, 5, 6

BEFORE

WHAT ARE YOU AWARE OF JUST NOW?
- ☐ My breathing
- ☐ My body
- ☐ My feelings
- ☐ My thoughts
- ☐ My actions

SELF-REFLECTION:

Slow your talking and listening

A recent research study looked at groups of people as they ate together. Both groups went out for a nice meal. Half the people were asked to not pick up their phones or use them. The other half could use them as normal. At the end everyone was asked to rate their experience of the meal. Those people who hadn't used their phones rated the conversation and experience as being far better, and more interesting, than those who had been interrupted again and again as they responded to social media, posting photos of their meals etc.

Practice the art of really listening. Listening so you can reflect on what's happening, and aware of your own inner talk and bodily sensations. Allow yourself to really notice and listen to those around you with openness and less judgement.

AFTER

WHAT ARE YOU AWARE OF JUST NOW? ☐ My breathing ☐ My body ☐ My feelings ☐ My thoughts ☐ My actions	SELF-REFLECTION:
	If things have altered, is this something you would like to plan to practice? Y ☐ N ☐

Skill 6

Slow down your life

MINDFUL WALKING

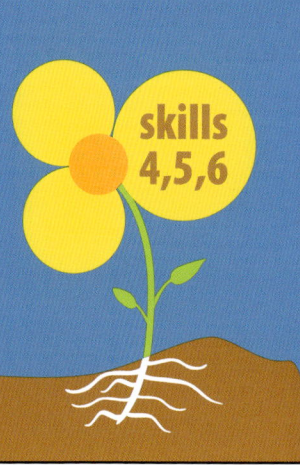

skills 4, 5, 6

BEFORE

WHAT ARE YOU AWARE OF JUST NOW?
- ☐ My breathing
- ☐ My body
- ☐ My feelings
- ☐ My thoughts
- ☐ My actions

SELF-REFLECTION:

Walking without purpose

The next step on from grounding, is to be aware of grounding while you're moving. Some people find mindful walking helpful, especially if you feel agitated and find it's difficult to settle.

We often walk automatically. How often have you arrived at a destination and have filled all the time looking downwards at a phone, on social media or thinking about all the things you have to do when you arrive?

Instead pay attention to your feet. Are they hot or cold? The pressure of the heel, the arch and the ball of your feet on the ground. Noticing your balance and movement. What is your mind making of this focus? Next consider your ankles and calves, and then allow your attention to move via your knees to your whole body.

Again we have prepared download resources to help you practice mindful walking.

To start with your surroundings may be a distraction. But with time you can expand out to observe the things around you as well.

Download from www.llttf.com/resources

AFTER	**WHAT ARE YOU AWARE OF JUST NOW?** ☐ My breathing ☐ My body ☐ My feelings ☐ My thoughts ☐ My actions	**SELF-REFLECTION:** If things have altered, is this something you would like to plan to practice? Y ☐ N ☐

* You will need to use your phone to play the recordings as you walk safely and mindfully.

Skill 7

Practice being kind...

...TO YOURSELF

skills 7,8,9

BEFORE

WHAT ARE YOU AWARE OF JUST NOW?
- ☐ My breathing
- ☐ My body
- ☐ My feelings
- ☐ My thoughts
- ☐ My actions

SELF-REFLECTION:

Become a better friend to yourself

Download from
www.llttf.com/resources

We are often kinder to others than ourselves. Take a step back and consider how you look after yourself. When something seems difficult or hard, what's the tone of how you speak to yourself? Encouraging and warm? Or critical and pulling down?

What would it be like if you let yourself off the hook of your own self-judgment and critical inner thoughts?

Most people just want to be happy, healthy and at ease. We would want that for someone we cared for such as a loved child. How can you allow yourself to experience this same kindness right now?

Practice recognising and choosing not to listen to the inner critic. Realising that life - and us as human beings - are imperfect. Instead accepting you are as you are - with all your strengths and weaknesses. Celebrating who you are and the journey you are on.

Like all living things, we flourish in an environment of warmth and kindness, rather than cold and criticism. How can you begin to be a little kinder to yourself? If you'd like to discover more about how to build kindness towards yourself, download the linked audio file.

AFTER

WHAT ARE YOU AWARE OF JUST NOW?
- ☐ My breathing
- ☐ My body
- ☐ My feelings
- ☐ My thoughts
- ☐ My actions

SELF-REFLECTION:

Skill 8

Practice being kind...

... TO OTHERS

skills 7,8,9

BEFORE	**WHAT ARE YOU AWARE OF JUST NOW?** ☐ My breathing ☐ My body ☐ My feelings ☐ My thoughts ☐ My actions	**SELF-REFLECTION:**

You started on the last two pages with being kinder and less judgmental to yourself. That helps us to grow and flourish. It can also be good for us to hold a similar attitude and action towards others.

Start by practicing kindness to the people in your life. Take it in steps.

1). To start with, choose someone you find it easy to be kind to. Perhaps someone who is kind to you and who you care about. Be aware of any harsh critical thoughts and judgments you have around that person. See what it might be like to wish that person well. They also wish to be happy, healthy and at ease just like you.

2). Others who you feel more neutral about. Practice developing a kindly attitude towards people in your life you don't know very well. The cashier in the supermarket, the postman or those sitting around you on the bus. They also wish to be safe and well. What might it be like to have a warm attitude towards each of them?

There are recordings for both these approaches available in the resources area.

Skill 8 continued over page...

Skill 8 (CONTINUED)

Practice being kind…

SHOWING KINDNESS TO ALL

3). Finally those who you find it currently challenging to accept and be kindly to. The mildly irritating people and also those who are difficult. Rather than judging, attacking or condemning them, how can you play around with, and change your attitude towards each of them. What about even the most difficult, challenging and rude people around us?

Experiment and see whether the shift to a friendlier attitude towards yourself helps you become more friendly to others too. **Task:** consider doing random acts of kindness to others.

For example, could you smile and say thank you at someone at the checkout? Or buy a cup of coffee for the person behind you in the queue? Or help an older person get their wheelie bin in and out? But also check if the random act is what the person actually wants.

AFTER

WHAT ARE YOU AWARE OF JUST NOW?	**SELF-REFLECTION:**
☐ My breathing ☐ My body ☐ My feelings ☐ My thoughts ☐ My actions	

Footnote: A friend of one of the authors paid for the toll fee for the car behind at a toll bridge. The confusion caused by the act led to a major traffic jam and congestion.

Skill 9

Practice being kind...

...BY SAYING THANK YOU

skills 7,8,9

BEFORE

WHAT ARE YOU AWARE OF JUST NOW?
- ☐ My breathing
- ☐ My body
- ☐ My feelings
- ☐ My thoughts
- ☐ My actions

SELF-REFLECTION:

Show your appreciation

Do we miss out on noticing the good things and people around us each and every day?

Look again at the things around you with fresh eyes. Do you notice what you **do** have - or what you **don't** have?

Have you ever noticed we are hardwired to notice the negatives - the threats, the things we don't have? We simply glide past the many positives in life each day. However, negative thoughts tend to stick in our brains and create a negative chemistry in the body. An attitude of gratitude helps us see the whole picture.

Choose to practice thankfulness towards the people and things in your life. Share that thankfulness with those around you. Say "thank you" to them, or "I really appreciate you" and see people's faces light up. Acknowledging others connects us, builds bonds and is an important form of kindness.

Skill 9 continued over page...

Skill 9 (CONTINUED)
Practice being kind...

GIVE ME FIVE

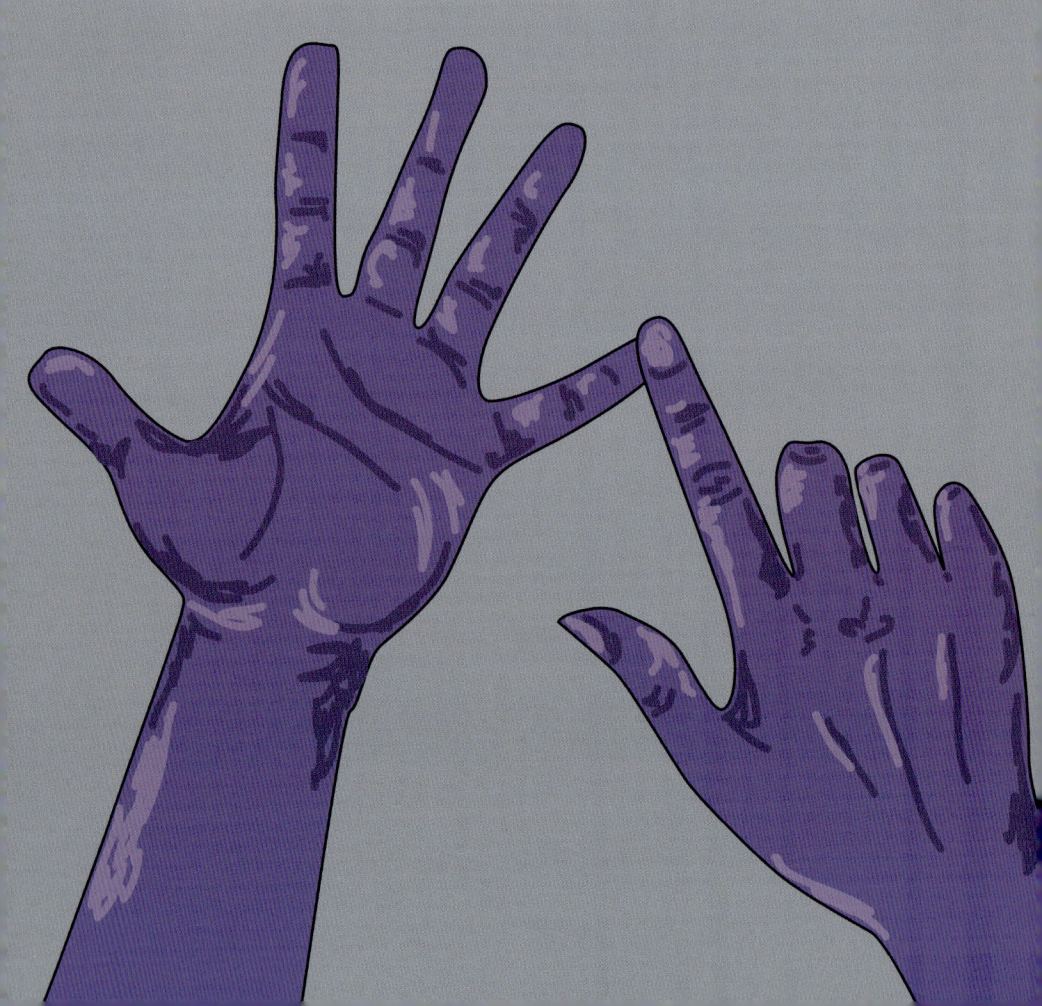

Use your fingers to remind you...

Bring to mind five simple things you are grateful for. It could be that first sip of tea in the morning, your cat, a caring family member, a sunset, a song. With your right hand hold on to your left thumb and bring to mind the first thing you are grateful for. Don't just think it - really allow yourself to feel gratitude in your body. Notice any sense of ease, warmth or any other sensations in your body.

By holding each finger in turn you have the chance to bring to mind one thing you are grateful for using each finger you hold.

AFTER

WHAT ARE YOU AWARE OF JUST NOW?
- ☐ My breathing
- ☐ My body
- ☐ My feelings
- ☐ My thoughts
- ☐ My actions

SELF-REFLECTION:

RECAP

9 WAYS TO LIVE LIFE MORE FULLY

Living fully in the now

Here's what you've learned so far.

Pay attention
1. Ground yourself
2. Focus on your breathing
3. Focus on your body

Slow down your life
4. Mindful eating
5. Mindful conversation
6. Mindful walking

Practice being kind
7. To yourself
8. To others
9. By saying thank you

And here's 3 final things to work on. They can bring mindfulness into your everyday life.

1 of 3 other important things

ASK YOURSELF WHAT BUILDS YOU UP AND WHAT PULLS YOU DOWN?

BEFORE

WHAT ARE YOU AWARE OF JUST NOW?
- ☐ My breathing
- ☐ My body
- ☐ My feelings
- ☐ My thoughts
- ☐ My actions

SELF-REFLECTION:

Now that you have developed an ability to notice what you need and bring kindness to yourself, you might also notice how circumstances in your life impact on your own inner sense of wellbeing. This offers you the opportunity to add some skillful choices to your life that lay strong roots for life.

By listening more clearly, bringing kindness to yourself and others and by being fully present in each moment you may notice all sorts of changes occur. It might be small changes - what you eat, what you listen to, and how you spend your time. So, if social media feeds you dissatisfaction of your own life compared to the selected images and posts of everyone else's "perfect" life, take a step back and look again at what and who you spend your time on.

How can you do less of what pulls you down, and do more of what adds joy to your life? Make any changes thoughtfully and in response to what you notice - not angrily, despairingly or reactively.

It's not about making sudden and impulsive decisions to storm out of a relationship or job. But it is about wise change.

AFTER

WHAT ARE YOU AWARE OF JUST NOW?
- [ ] My breathing
- [ ] My body
- [ ] My feelings
- [ ] My thoughts
- [ ] My actions

SELF-REFLECTION:

2 of 3 other important things

LOOK AT THE WORLD AROUND YOU WITH FRESH EYES

BEFORE

WHAT ARE YOU AWARE OF JUST NOW?
- ☐ My breathing
- ☐ My body
- ☐ My feelings
- ☐ My thoughts
- ☐ My actions

SELF-REFLECTION:

When someone recovers from serious illness ...

... they often start to see things they have taken for granted through new eyes. Do you remember when you were young and it was autumn? Perhaps we might have come across a pile of leaves in the garden, jump in them and play. But when we get older we start to get sensible, and take everything for granted. But why wait for sudden serious illness to make us step back and value the things around us?

Go outside.
- Ground yourself (Steps 1-3). Feel the air on your skin. The warmth of the sun on your face, or the coolness of the air or rain on your skin.
- Reach out and notice the textures of plants, trees or whatever is there.
- Breathe in, notice any smells or even flavours in the air.
- Listen.
- Look around. Notice the vibrant colours, the shapes of the vegetation and any animals that might be around.
- Become fully present wherever you are.

AFTER

WHAT ARE YOU AWARE OF JUST NOW?	SELF-REFLECTION:
☐ My breathing ☐ My body ☐ My feelings ☐ My thoughts ☐ My actions	

3 of 3
other important things

TURN TOWARDS YOUR DIFFICULTIES

BEFORE

WHAT ARE YOU AWARE OF JUST NOW?
- ☐ My breathing
- ☐ My body
- ☐ My feelings
- ☐ My thoughts
- ☐ My actions

SELF-REFLECTION:

We often choose to avoid things that seem scary. That's understandable. However the problem is that when we avoid things it makes us feel better in the short term, but our lives get smaller. To really live life fully we can choose to do things that expand our life. Things that make it a little bit bigger rather than smaller. And then be mindful and take joy from those things you do.

How could you begin to respond differently to any unhelpful thoughts that say you won't enjoy something, or when you guess that no-one will talk to you? Or that you'll have nothing to say or mess things up? How can you get to build confidence? What you'd advise someone else is to do things one step at a time. Be gentle to yourself and take things slowly, trusting your own inner wisdom. Plan activities that move you forward. Each step should be big enough to improve things, but not so large they seem daunting, or are so hard you struggle and fail.

Remember change is all about making wise choices. With the support of the mindfulness practices that you've learned, you'll be more aware of your inner growth and stability as it happens.

AFTER

| **WHAT ARE YOU AWARE OF JUST NOW?**
☐ My breathing
☐ My body
☐ My feelings
☐ My thoughts
☐ My actions | **SELF-REFLECTION:** |

HANG ON - MAYBE YOU FIND MINDFULNESS TRICKY?

If you're struggling with the mindfulness approach suggested so far, it may be there are other things you can bring mindfulness to.

For example, are there other activities in your life that you know already are helpful to you?

Get active:
- Go for a walk or run.
- Swimming.
- Skiing.
- Rock climbing.

Get focused:
- Craft work.
- Knitting.
- Playing a musical instrument.
- Fix something.
- Play an online game.

Get social:
- Attend a group that interests you.
- Invite people round for a chat or banter.
- Spend time with people you like.

Or anything that works for you.

BEFORE YOU FINISH

Here's a reminder of the qualities you want to grow

Helping you flourish

We have tried to teach these key principles of mindfulness throughout the book. They are attitudes that will help you grow.

- Not trying to get things right.
- If your mind wanders don't beat yourself up - gently bring it back to your focus.
- Practice is useful in it's own right.
- Becoming more patient with yourself.
- Slowing and not rushing through each moment of the day doing, doing, doing.
- Practice accepting things as they are right now - that way you have a starting point from which to make wise choices.
- Gaining understanding offers clarity of how you and others actually are.
- Could self-compassion and kindness underpin your life?
- Trusting yourself and your own experiences and intuition.
- Openness and curiosity can allow you to be open to learn new ways of living.
- Exploring and learning using an attitude of experimentation and discovery.
- Letting go of things that pull you down.
- Watching out for times when you cling on to things because it feels comfortable even when they are no longer helpful.
- Looking at things with fresh eyes each day.

To find out more about mindfulness approaches

WHERE TO GET EVEN MORE HELP

For more tips on feeling better, go to www.llttf.com. It's free and the number one site for low mood and anxiety recommended by NHS Trusts and teams in England.* It's packed with ways to lift your mood and start having a happier and healthier life.

There are links on there so you can connect with other people who are making changes to their lives too.

*Bennion et al, 2017. BMJ Open http://bmjopen.bmj.com/content/7/1/e014844